ALADDIN AND THE WONDERFUL LAMP

by

JAMES NORRIS

Royalty Note

The possession of this book without a written authorization first having been obtained from the publisher, confers no right or license to professionals or amateurs to produce the play publicly or in private for gain or charity.

In its present form, this play is dedicated to the reading public only, and not to producers. However, productions of this play are encouraged, and those who wish to present it may secure the necessary permission by writing to The Children's Theatre Press, Anchorage, Kentucky.

This play may be presented by amateurs, upon payment to The Children's Theatre Press, of a royalty of $15.00 for each performance, one week before the date the play is to be given. This play is fully protected by copyright, and anyone presenting it without the consent of The Children's Theatre Press, will be liable to the penalties by law provided.

Whenever the play is produced, the following notice must appear on all programmes, printing, and advertising for the play: "Produced by special arrangement with The Children's Theatre Press, of Anchorage, Kentucky".

2

PEOPLE OF THE PLAY

ALADDIN

HIS MOTHER

THE PRINCESS BADROULBADOUR, nicknamed "Adora"

THE SULTAN, her father

NOONA, her attendant

AFRICAN MAGICIAN

THE GENIE OF THE RING

THE GENIE OF THE LAMP

KEELO
BARAKA
BALSORA
ZURINA   } Slaves of the ring
CARLAMON
OLANA

SLAVES OF THE LAMP (four parts which can be doubled)

KALISSA, a neighbor of Aladdin's

A GUARD

CITIZENS

SYNOPSIS

ACT ONE
>   SCENE 1. A glen outside the city at mid-day.
>   SCENE 2. Inside the magic cave.

ACT TWO
>   SCENE 1. The glen agan, at dusk.
>   SCENE 2. The glen again, by moonlight.

ACT THREE
>   Inside the Princess' Palace.

This play was first performed by the Goodman Theatre, of Chicago, Illinois, under the direction of Charlotte B. Chorpenning.

Aladdin and the Wonderful Lamp

ACT ONE

SCENE 1: *A glen, outside the city. In the background is a large rock, and beyond a suggestion of trees. In the distance, the roof-tops of the city are seen. In the top of the rock is a square stone with a large brass ring in it. It must be hidden from the view of the audience till seen in the course of the action. When the stone is lifted, it must leave an opening large enough for one person to enter. The curtain rises on an empty stage. It is mid-day.*

MOTHER *(off)*: Aladdin! Aladdin! Where on earth can that boy be? Aladdin! *(She enters, searching everywhere.)* Ah me, that boy will be the death of me yet. ALADDIN!! If his father were still alive, he wouldn't run away like this. Sometimes I wish I had a daughter instead of a son. Girls are much easier to manage than boys . . . Aladdin!!!

(She exits down left, her voice fading away. Aladdin enters down right. He leaps to the top of the rock in the foreground and laughs loudly as his mother's voice becomes fainter.)

ALADDIN: A rooster perched on a rock by the road.
He flapped his wings and loundly crowed,
Oo—Hoo—ooh—Hoo—Hooo!!

(He flaps his hands to his sides and crows like a rooster. A young girl enters down left, running and looking about eagerly. She stops dead as she hears a man's voice calling in the distance. Aladdin sees her and hides behind the rock. The girl looks in the direction of the voice and hides behind the other end of the rock.)

SULTAN *(off)*: Adora—Adora!!

(He enters left, with Noona and a guard.)

Adora—Adora!! Find her, I tell you. Find her at once. Ohhhhhh—Woe is me. I know misfortune will come to her. ADORA!!! *(To guard:)* You will be beaten for this, my good man. Why did you let her out of your sight?

GUARD: I didn't let her out of my sight, Sultan. She was walking down the street as gentle as you please. I was holding her hand and she bade me let it go, but I refused. Whereupon, she sank her little teeth into my little finger and before I knew it, she was gone.

SULTAN: Oh, my little pigeon, you will drive me to my grave. I do my best to give her everything she wants to make her happy. I give her dresses of the finest silk. Everything she touches is of the purest gold. She has the finest pet elephant in all the world. Even his harness is inlaid with the rarest of stones from all over the earth. But she will not stay home with them. She's always running away. And why? WHY???

NOONA *(shaking her head solemnly)*: She says she wants to see the world. She wants to see what other boys and girls are like.

SULTAN: If I catch any boys or girls with her, I'll lock them in the tower. Ahhhh—sometimes I wish she had been a boy. Boys are much less trouble. ADORA!!!

(He exits with Noona and the Guard, still calling. Aladdin's head appears from behind one end of the rock, and Adora's very cautiously from the other. They listen a moment.)

ADORA *(suddenly seeing Aladdin)*: Oh . . . was it you who did that funny crow?

ALADDIN *(nodding and grinning)*: Shall I do it again?

ADORA: Do it softly. They might hear you.

ALADDIN: Ooo—HOO—Hoo—OO—Hoo!

ADORA: Ooo—HOO—OOH—hOO—oooH!

(They both laugh.)

What's your name?

ALADDIN: Aladdin. What's yours?

ADORA: My real name's Badroulbadour, but my father calls me Adora.

ALADDIN: Oh, what a funny name.

ADORA: It's not any funnier than yours.

ALADDIN: Where do you live?

ADORA: I live in the Palace on the hill.

ALADDIN: Why, that's the Sultan's Palace!

ADORA: I ought to know that. He's my father.

ALADDIN: Ohh—are you the Princess?

ADORA: Yes. I'm hiding from my father.

ALADDIN: I'm hiding from my mother.

ADORA: Is she unkind to you?

ALADDIN: Oh no! She's a good woman and very kind. She just doesn't understand me.

ADORA: My father thinks he gives me everything I want, but he never lets me out of the Palace. It's very lonely. Do you have to stay at home too?

ALADDIN: Oh, no. It's much more fun to go about the city.

ADORA: Do you live far from here?

ALADDIN: No, look. You can see the top of our tailor shop from here.

ADORA: Oh, I've never seen a tailor shop. I wish I could see it inside.

ALADDIN: You can. Come with me.

ADORA: Aren't you afraid to take me with you?

6

ALADDIN (*grinning*):   No.

ADORA: You heard what my father said. If he catches you with me, he'll shut you up in the tower.

ALADDIN: He won't catch me.

(*The Magician enters stealthily. He gives a low sinister chuckle. He looks toward the rock. The children crowd close together, watching him.*)

ADORA: What a strange looking old man! I wish he wouldn't star at us so. Let's leave him.

ALADDIN: There's nothing to be afraid of.

ADORA: I'm not afraid. I just want to go to your shop.

(*They move down right, and Aladdin stops and turns to Adora.*)

ALADDIN (*ceremoniously*):   Does her Highness wish to ride the black horse or the white one?

(*Adora at first looks puzzled and surprised, then enters into the spirit of the thing. They pantomine.*)

ADORA: I shall ride the white horse, thank you.

ALADDIN: Very well, your ladyship. He is a very trusty steed. (*He pantomimes helping her on one horse and then pretends to mount the other. They both grab imaginary bridles.*)   All ready?

ADORA: Ready.

ALADDIN: We're off!

(*They pantomine a lusty gallop and exit laughing.*)

MAGICIAN: Little brats! (*He goes up onto the rock and searches about. He seems to find what he was looking for.*)   At last my journey is ended. (*He bends down as if to lift something, then straightens up.*)   No one must know. No one must know.

(*He scrambles down off the rock, assures himself that he is unseen, then gets back up on it quickly. He kneels, scrapes away dirt and pulls at the slab of rock with all his might. It is immovable. He goes over backward in his efforts, yet it does not move. Finally he sits down with his legs under him, removes a huge ring from his finger, holds it into the light, and rubs it. With a rumble of thunder, and a change of lights, the Genie of the Ring appears.*)

GENIE: What wouldst thou? I am thy slave and the slave of all who wear the ring. I must obey. I and the other slaves of the ring.

MAGICIAN: Am I truly at the end of my journey? Is this the rock that covers the cave where the magic lamp is burning?

GENIE: You are at the end of your journey.

MAGICIAN: Then lift this rock that I cannot lift. Open to me this cave. Haste, lest someone come and discover it also.

GENIE: That I cannot do.

MAGICIAN: Have you brought me to the very entrance of the magic cave, only to tell me you cannot open it?

GENIE: I can open it, but not for you.

MAGICIAN: Are you not my slave?

7

GENIE: I must obey you in all things that follow the laws of the ring. But he who enters this cave must follow the laws of the Lamp.

MAGICIAN: I will obey, good Genie. What are the laws of the Lamp?

GENIE: The slaves of the Lamp cannot obey anyone who has greed in his soul.

MAGICIAN: I have no greed, good Genie.

GENIE: You stop at nothing to get what you want for yourself. You caused the death of your own brother because you wanted the magic spells he used. You want this Lamp for your own gain. The cave will never open at your word, Magician.

MAGICIAN: Is there no way by which I can get this lamp? *(He turns the ring.)* It will give its owner untold power. *(Turning ring.)* Is there no way? *(Turning ring.)* Is there no way? Thou art my slave. Answer.

GENIE *(unwillingly)*: I am your slave and the slave of all who wear the ring. There is a way. There is a way.

MAGICIAN: Tell me. Tell me what it is.

GENIE You must find some one else to enter the cave for you. Some one who is fit to touch the lamp.

MAGICIAN: But who? Who? How shall I know who is fit?

GENIE: He who would enter this cave must know how to imagine things that are not for his own greed.

MAGICIAN: Every one can imagine things.

GENIE: Every one can imagine things, but few can imagine things without greed.

MAGICIAN: How can I find such a person? I could never tell if he was the right one.

GENIE *(triumphantly)*: That's because you cannot imagine such things yourself.

MAGICIAN: Is there no way for me to find out who can do it? *He twists the ring.)* Is there no way?

GENIE *(writhing)*: There is a way.

MAGICIAN: Tell it to me. Tell it to me.

GENIE: You must ask him a certain question.

MAGICIAN: What is it? Tell me quickly—

GENIE: Ask him this—*(pause.)* "What is a circle?"

MAGICIAN: A circle? That is easy. "What is a circle?" And what must his answer be?

GENIE: If he names things that are made by man, he cannot imagine anything except his own greed. If he names things that are not made by man, he can imagine other things, and is fit to touch the Lamp. Magic and imagination go hand in hand.

MAGICIAN: And when I find such a person, what shall I do then?

GENIE *(handing two sticks)*: Give him these two sticks. Command him to rub them together and say the name of his father three times. When the smoke is cleared away, you will see a large brass ring in this rock. Bid him lift it and it shall come to pass.

MAGICIAN: All this I can do. Farewell, good Genie.

(Thunder and change of lights. The Genie disappears.)

I shall find such a one. I will be more powerful than anyone on earth! I shall be the lord of the universe and make the world dance to the crack of my whip! I will defy the Sultan and carry off his daughter! *(He laughs to himself, triumphantly. Aladdin's mother enters with Kalissa, a neighbor woman, both searching for Aladdin.)* What is a circle? I shall ask everyone I meet until I find the right one.

KALISSA: It was here I saw him a while ago.

MAGICIAN: Good morning, friends. I'd like to put a question to you.

MOTHER: Put it freely.

MAGICIAN: What is a circle?

BOTH: A circle? A circle?

MOTHER: He jests.

KALISSA: Come along.

MAGICIAN *(holding up a silver piece)*: If you can tell me what a circle is, I'll give you this piece of silver.

MOTHERS: Why, a plate of food. That is a circle.

KALISSA: The bottom of my rice jar.

MOTHER: The top of a wine cask—

KALISSA: And that piece of silver is a circle! Now give it to me.

MOTHER: No, it is mine—

(She reaches for it and he snatches it back. Between them they drop it. Kalissa puts her foot on it behind their backs as they turn and twist looking for it. If she has to dash some distance to do this, all the better.)

Now, you see. You have lost my silver piece.

MAGICIAN: You had no right to try to take it.

MOTHER: It's mine. You promised it. I'm going to take it when I find it.

(They hunt at length, first one and then the other thinking he sees it and dashing for it. followed by the other. Kalissa tries again and again to stoop down and get it from under her foot, but is always checked by their looking around before her motion is complete. At last they catch her.)

BOTH: You!!

MAGICIAN: You are a thief—

MOTHER: Good neighbor, lift your foot. It is on my silver piece.

(Kalissa turns on the silver piece as on a pivot, lifts her foot, etc.)

KALISSA: What do you say? *(She shoves the silver piece over with her foot so as to change her position and seems to be looking for it.)* Where is it, then?

MAGICIAN *(to himself)*: It's a good thing they didn't either of them give the right answer. They would have stolen the lamp when I sent them down for it. *(To them:)* I'm glad you stole the silver. It

9

has taught me to make sure the person I am looking for is honest. Go along home, the two of you. You'll neither of you do.

KALISSA *(who has picked up the silver)*: I'm going. Nobody would want to stay where you are.

MOTHER: I want the silver piece. I need it for food.

MAGICIAN: Make her give it to you. She has it.

(The mother rushes off after Kalissa. The Magician climbs onto the rock.)

I must cover the rock till I come back. No one must know.

(He throws the dirt back on. He starts off as he hears Aladdin and Adora laughing.)

Two of them. I must watch my chance and test them one at a time.

(Magician crosses furtively to one side to wait for his opportunity. Aladdin and Adora enter, laughing.)

ADORA: A tailor's shop is a very funny place. It's so little. And all cut out of wood.

ALADDIN: It must seem very poor when you've always lived in a palace of gold.

ADORA: You can feel poor in a palace of gold, too. Sometimes people get lost in our palace. It's so big. And it's very lonely. I often wish I could have a palace of my very own—one much smaller than my father's—the kind you can be happy in.

ALADDIN: I hope you get your little palace, Princess. Then maybe I could come to visit you some time.

ADORA: You'd always be welcome in my little palace.

SULTAN *(off)*: Adora! ADORA!!

ADORA: Hide!

(Aladdin runs behind the rock. He sneezes.)

Don't do that. He'll find you.

ALADDIN *(sneezing again)*: I can't help it.

ADORA: Wait for me here. I'll go home with them now, but I'll come back as soon as my father's back is turned.

ALADDIN: We'll go to the fountain where all the children swim.

ADORA: Oh . . . I've never been there!

ALADDIN: I can dive from the highest statue.

ADORA: They're almost here. Good-bye. *(She crows very softly. Aladdin crows very faintly, his head sticking out from behind the rock.)* Good-bye . . .

(Enter the Sultan, Noona and the Guard.)

SULTAN: There she is!

NOONA: Where have you been, Princess?

SULTAN *(as Adora grins)*: She doesn't care a bit. *(Booming:)* Where have you been?

ADORA: I've been looking at the city, father. It's beautiful.

SULTAN: Our palace is the most beautiful thing in the city. Why don't you stay home and look at *it?*

ADORA: Have you been to the fountain where all the children swim, father?

SULTAN: So that's where you've been. *(To guard, bellowing:)* You've let her go about the city all by herself. You'll be flogged for this.

ADORA: I haven't been to the fountain yet, father. And I wasn't all by myself. A boy was with me.

SULTAN: A boy? Who? Why? A boy of the streets with you! Where is he? Where is he?

ADORA: Oh—He—he—he isn't with me any more.

SULTAN: Guard! Before nightfall, find this boy and bring him to me. To dare to lead the great Princess through the dirty streets. Find him, I tell you!

(Aladdin sneezes behind the rock. They all jump.)

What on earth was that?

ADORA: Did—did you sneeze, Noona? *(pause)* You just sneezed, didn't you, Noona, dear?

NOONA: Ah—why—yes, Princess, I must have sneezed.

ADORA: I'll be good now, father.

(Aladdin sneezes again. Adora hears the start of it and jogs Noona, who sneezes loudly to cover it.)

SULTAN: There's someone sneezing behind that rock.

ADORA: I'll be very good, father. I'll look at our palace as much as you want me to.

(The Sultan starts toward the rock. Adora nudges Noona frantically.)

NOONA: Would your Majesty care to have Noona look behind the rock?

SULTAN: Away with you, woman. I'll look for myself.

(He goes to one end of the rock and Aladdin's head appears at the other. The Sultan starts toward the other end and Adora motions Aladdin frantically. He disappears.)

I don't like people sneezing behind my back.

(He tries the other end of the rock and Aladdin appears at the other.)

I don't see anybody. This is very strange.

(He now circles around the rock, Aladdin always managing to keep out of his sight with the help of pantomine instructions from Adora. After circling the rock four or five times, the Sultan gives up.)

Come along home, Princess. Your old father is very tired. If you wish to look at the city, Ali will take you for a ride on your pet elephant. You'd like that, wouldn't you?

ADORA: Yes, father.

(They leave, backs to the rock. At the farthest end of it stands Aladdin. He looks horror-stricken as he tries to suppress a sneeze. He presses a finger on his upper lip, but cannot control it. Finally after the Sultan is off, he sneezes subdued under his hand. He is apprehensive and very still. From off stage comes a faint crow. He laughs and answers it. The Magician comes out from his hiding place.)

MAGICIAN: Good day to you, my son.

11

ALADDIN: Good day, sir.

MAGICIAN: I wonder if you would be so kind as to give me some small silver pieces in exchange for this piece of gold.

ALADDIN: I'm sorry, sir, but I cannot. I haven't even one piece of silver.

MAGICIAN (delighted): I'm sorry to hear that you are so poor. Perhaps I could help you to earn some money.

ALADDIN: Oh, I'm very strong, and I can run faster than anyone in the city my own age.

MAGICIAN: The thing I want you to do is easy, yet it will take skill.

ALADDIN: I'm a good swimmer, too.

MAGICIAN: Do you know the house of Houssain, the merchant?

ALADDIN: Yes, I know it well. I used to play by the wall that goes around his lane.

MAGICIAN: Very good. I have tried in vain to get into his house but the guards will not let me through the gates. You are young and strong, and could easily climb the wall. Then you can fasten a rope and so make it possible for me to enter the grounds. Now, isn't that an easy way to earn two shiny pieces of silver?

ALADDIN: 'Tis easy enough, sir. But old Houssain would not like anyone to sneak into his house that way.

MAGICIAN: He stole a precious heirloom from my family and will not give it back. All you have to do is go to the top of the wall. There is no harm in that. Two shiny pieces of silver—
(He shows the coins to Aladdin and rubs them together.)

ALADDIN: Old Houssain is an honest merchant and I don't believe you. Climb the wall yourself. And I hope you fall and break your neck.

MAGICIAN (delighted): Heh, heh, heh, heh—

ALADDIN: You needn't laugh at me.

MAGICIAN: I am laughing with joy, my son. I am happy to see you will not stoop to a dishonest deed for a few pieces of silver.

ALADDIN: Then why did you ask me to do it?

MAGICIAN: Only to test you, my son.

ALADDIN: Oh, you were just fooling me.

MAGICIAN: I have a secret adventure which I may entrust to you. I am glad to see you are an honest boy.

ALADDIN: I have never thought about being honest.

MAGICIAN: Honest people don't. I have a question to ask of you, my son. Do you know what a circle is?

ALADDIN: Of course I do.

MAGICIAN (eagerly): What is it?

ALADDIN: Don't you know?

MAGICIAN: Eh? Oh yes, my boy, yes indeed. But I wish to find out if you know.

ALADDIN: You're a very funny man. Are you trying to fool me again?

12

MAGICIAN: No, my son. No. What is a circle?

ALADDIN: The moon is a circle. The sun is a circle. If I stand up like this and someone tied a string to the end of this finger and stretched it all the way around the world and tied the other end to this finger, it would make a circle. I think the inside of my head is a circle somewhere, but I don't know where.

(He giggles uproariously, whirls around on one leg and sits with his hands folded across his knees.)

MAGICIAN: By all the gods, you must be the right one!

ALADDIN: What do you mean, "the right one"?

MAGICIAN: Do as I say and you can become richer than the greatest monarch in the world.

ALADDIN: Nobody would want to be so rich.

MAGICIAN: Think of the nice things you could buy for your mother and father.

ALADDIN: My father is dead, but my mother likes nice things. She works very hard just to get enough to eat. I'd like to get nice things for her.

MAGICIAN: You can.

ALADDIN: Are you fooling me again?

MAGICIAN: Listen and you shall see. Beneath this rock is a cave, which contains a hidden treasure. I am forbidden to open the cave or to set foot in it when it is opened. You are the one to open the cave. You are the one to enter and bring up the treasure. Are you afraid?

ALADDIN: I am not. What must I do, sir?

MAGICIAN: Take these two sticks.

ALADDIN: Yes, sir.

MAGICIAN: Take them to the top of the big rock.

ALADDIN *(on rock)*: Here they are, sir. What next?

MAGICIAN: Rub the stocks together hard. Repeat the name of your father three times.

ALADDIN *(rubbing sticks)*: Mustapha-Mustapha-Mustapha!

(There is a blast of blue smoke, and a zoooooom!! Aladdin runs down the rock.)

MAGICIAN: Do not be afraid, my son. Look.

ALADDIN: I am not afraid. But I was a little surprised.

MAGICIAN: We have uncovered the entrance to the cave. This large stone is covering it.

ALADDIN: What's the big brass ring for?

MAGICIAN: You are to lift the stone by it.

ALADDIN: I'm as strong as anyone in the city my age, but it would take a giant to lift that rock.

MAGICIAN: You think so, my son. Again you must pronounce the name of your father three times. Then you take hold of the ring.

ALADDIN: Mustapha—Mustapha—Mustapha!

13

(He lifts the stone with ease and a flood of light comes through the opening of the cave.)

Oh, it's all shiny down there. This is truly a wonderful adventure, sir. Now what do we do?

MAGICIAN: Place the stone very near the edge, my son. It will be easier to put back in place if it balances its own weight.

ALADDIN: Like this?

MAGICIAN: Yes, my son. That's just right. Anyone could move it now.

ALADDIN: Now, what do I do?

MAGICIAN: You must go down these steps alone. At the bottom you will find four large brass vessels, full of gold and silver. Take care that you do not meddle with them.

ALADDIN: Of course not. They aren't mine.

MAGICIAN: You will come into a large room, the like of which no man has ever seen. There will be trees, laden with jewels and golden fruit. You may gather as much as you please. But take care you are not so carried away with the wonders of the cave that you forget your task and lose your way.

ALADDIN: What is my task?

MAGICIAN: Somewhere in the cave you will find a niche, and in this niche a lighted lamp. Take the lamp down and put the light out. Throw the wick away and pour out the liquid. Then bring the lamp to me.

ALADDIN: I'll go at once, sir, before I forget all you've told me.

MAGICIAN: Go at once, and boldly, my son.

(Aladdin climbs into the opening.)

MAGICIAN: Farewell, my son!

(Aladdin starts down into the cave, then looks back up at the Magician.)

ALADDIN: Are you sure it's safe?

MAGICIAN: Reach your hand up. This is a magic ring and will keep you from harm till you bring the lamp back to me.

(Magician places the ring on Aladdin's hand. Aladdin giggles with excitement and quickly ducks out of sight.)

At last, my labours are ended. I will be the richest man in the world.

MOTHER *(voice off stage, faintly)*: Aladdin! Aladdin! Aladdin!

(Magician lifts his hands above his head in triumph, and his silhouette makes sinister shadows as the light coming up from the cave reveals it. His laughter builds as the curtain falls.)

CURTAIN

ACT ONE

SCENE 2: *Inside the cave. The cave is all shining with glitter and colored lights. There are trees with gold and silver fruits. There must be one down right and one up center. Steps up left of center lead directly to the opening of the cave, which is above curtain line, and out of sight. There are passages leading out of the cave, low, high, as desired. Urns of coin are on either side of the steps. Center back is a niche, containing a lamp which is burned low. The light from the sun above pours into the cave where the steps disappear upward. This makes the lamp appear very inconspicuous. There is a slight pause and one by one of the slaves of the ring appear. They advance toward the entrance of the cave with their hands uplifted.*

KEELO: We are here, oh Genie of the ring!

ALL: We the slaves of the ring are here!

CARLAMON: What is your will, great Genie?

ALL: What is your will?

BARAKA: Our master does not answer us.

ZURINA: Perhaps he is angry with us.

OLANA: The old Magician turned the ring. I felt it turn.

BALSORA: I, too. His hand was trembling as it turned.

KEELO: Perhaps he didn't turn it hard enough.

CARLAMON: I hope that's true. I hate to do the bidding of the old Magician.

ZURINA: I hate it too.

BARAKA: Quick—someone is coming!

OLANA: Who could it be?

KEELO: Out of sight. He'll see us. Hurry! Hurry!

(*They all rush quickly and hide. They peep around the corners a moment and disappear as Aladdin comes down the steps. He is overcome with the wonder of the cave. He calls to the Magician who is out of sight.*)

ALADDIN: Ohhhhh—I never saw anything like this before.

MAGICIAN (*off*): Don't be afraid, my son.

ALADDIN: I'm not afraid. I—I—I'm just not used to it.

MAGICIAN: Get the lamp and bring it to me.

ALADDIN: There are many doors and openings. There must be other rooms. Which one has the lamp?

MAGICIAN: What?

ALADDIN: Which room has the lamp?

MAGICIAN: I don't know. You must find it.

ALADDIN: I will. I will! (*He comes down slowly, still in wonder.*

15

He grins and giggles with delight as he goes to examine the tree.)
I wish Adora could be here. *(He starts to pick some fruit.)* He
said I could. But I'd better find the lamp first.
*(He goes from one entrance to the other and peers into each one. He
then puts his hands over his eyes and pantomimes "Eenie Meenie,
Minie, Mo," with the other hand and disappears into the entrance
he is pointing to when he finishes. He giggles as he exits. The slaves
of the ring enter and look after him. They are of various ages and
builds and should be selected so as to make an interesting "verse
choir.")*

KEELO: The ring was on his finger. I saw it.

ZURINA: The Magician must have given it to him.

BARAKA: Do you know what that means? No more shall we do the
bidding of the old Magician.

OLANA: The slaves of the ring shall do the bidding of a young boy.

CARLAMON *(leaping part way up the steps and shaking a fist upward)*:
We'll never obey you again, old Magician—never!

ALL: Never again. Never!

BALSORA: No more of his wicked commands.

BARAKA: No more of his cruel deeds must we help him do.

CARLAMON *(again shaking his fist toward the entrance to the cave)*:
No more greedy wishes shall we bring to pass for you!
*(The light which comes through the entrance to the cave begins to
narrow. Carlamon leaps up toward it. It widens and narrows again.)*
(Carlamon leans toward the others): The Magician is ploting evil
against Aladdin.

BARAKA: What is he doing!

CARLAMON: He is lifting and lowering the rock that hides the opening
to the cave.
(The shaft of light stops moving.)

ZURINA *(running up another step)*: He's muttering to himself.

KEELO: What does he say?

ZURINA: He says—"This hole is large enough to get the lamp through.
But Aladdin can't get through, himself."
(There is a moment's silence. Pictures of slaves listening intently.)

BARAKA: What does he say now?

CARLAMON: He is laughing.
(The slaves are angered at this. Another silence.)

BALSORA: What does he say now?

ZURINA: He is silent.
(They listen.)

CARLAMON: He is waiting for Aladdin.

OLANA: What do you think the Magician will do to Aladdin?

BARAKA: He made Aladdin balance the rock so he can move it himself.
As soon he gets the lamp in his hands he will push the big rock
over the entrance to the cave and Aladdin will be a prisoner. He

16

will never get out.

KEELO: His mother will never know where he has gone.

BARAKA: No one will know.

CARLAMON: We will help him. We must help him.

KEELO: Aladdin wears the ring. We are his slaves. We can open the cave for him.

ZURINA: The Magician didn't tell him how to use the ring.

OLANA: Doesn't he know he must turn the ring if he needs us?

BARAKA: He doesn't even know about us.

CARLAMON: We can do nothing to help him unless he turns the ring.

ZURINA: Oh—If only we could tell him to turn it. We must find a way to make him call us.

KEELO: Let us try the ritual of the ring. Aladdin was fit to enter the cave. Maybe we can reach him by magic.

CARLAMON: Yes! Yes! Let us fill the cave with the magic of the ritual. Maybe we can make him turn the ring without his knowing it.

(They take places on their knees in a circle.)

BARAKA: Be quick, before he comes back.

CARLAMON: Sovereign Guide to whom we pray—

ALL: Sovereign Guide—Sovereign Guide—

CARLAMON: Who maketh night and the light of day—

ALL: Sovereign Guide—Sovereign Guide—

BARAKA: Harken to us while we sing—

ALL: And make the emblem of the ring!

(They turn palms up and out and repeat "Sovereign Guide, Sovereign Guide." They have said this in a very low voice. As they get to their feet, the left hand is placed on the shoulder of the one in front, forming a circle. The heads move up and down as they start moving slowly. A lobsterscope may be used to give the effect of speed. During this the right hand moves in a circular motion. As they go around they repeat the following:)

ALL *(or different voices)*: The world is a circle. The sun is a circle. The ring is a circle—round and around and around and around!

(They continue this chant through the rest of the ritual. They all kneel in formation with heads bowed on the shoulder of the one in front with right arms forming a circle about them as the lobsterscope stops. A concentrated color spot picks them up. A noise is heard from Aladdin, and they break. The lights come up.)

CARLAMON: He is coming. Out of sight—all of you!

(They hide. Aladdin enters. His arms are full of gold and jeweled fruits. He suddenly sees the lamp and starts to giggle.)

ALADDIN: Oh—there it is! Right near the steps. Well—it's a very small lamp.

(He takes the lamp but drops fruit in his efforts. He puts the lamp back, puts the fruit on the ground or steps, takes the lamp again, pulls out the wick and pours out the oil.)

It's just an ordinary lamp.

(He puts the fruit in his blouse, then changes his mind. He takes it out and puts the lamp in, then the fruit.)

I'd better put the lamp in first so I won't lose it. I know Adora hasn't any of this shiny fruit in her palace. She'll be very surprised.

(He starts up the steps, then goes back to one of the trees and picks a few more fruits. His blouse is very full.)

I look so fat. Adora would never know me.

(He throws out his chest and crows loudly. Then he goes on up. He stops just in sight of the audience, a shaft of light on his face.)

I'm coming up, sir. Are you there, sir?

MAGICIAN *(off)*: I am here. Have you got the lamp, my son?

ALADDIN: Yes. I have it. It's a very little lamp, sir.

MAGICIAN: You have done well, my son. Come up a little nearer.

ALADDIN: Open the hole a little wider, sir. I'm all stuffed out with shiny fruits and I couldn't get through there.

MAGICIAN: Reach me the lamp first and it will be easier for you to get through.

ALADDIN: I can't get to it. I put it at the bottom of my blouse so I wouldn't lose it.

MAGICIAN: Take the fruit out.

ALADDIN:. You told me I could have the fruit.

MAGICIAN: Do as I tell you.

ALADDIN: Why can't I bring the fruit and the lamp together?

MAGICIAN: Reach me the lamp.

ALADDIN: Give me more room and I'll come out with it.

MAGICIAN: Give me the lamp first, I tell you!

ALADDIN: I told you I couldn't. I'll give it to you as soon as I get out.

MAGICIAN: I'll let you out, my son. Just reach me the lamp and you'll see.

ALADDIN: I don't believe you.

MAGICIAN: How dare you defy the great Magician. How dare you!

ALADDIN: I'll get out by myself. I will!! I WILL!!!

MAGICIAN: Don't come a step higher till you've reached me the lamp.

ALADDIN: Get away from the cave or I'll knock you head over heels!

(He goes up the steps till only his legs show. They are planted far apart.)

MAGICIAN *(booming)*: Get back, you young ruffian! Get back, I tell you!

ALADDIN: Get out of my way!

MAGICIAN: You will, will you? Defy me, will you? I'll teach you—take that, you young—

ALADDIN: Stop pushing me—STOP!!! STOP!!!

(He comes tumbling down the steps, pulls himself together and rushes up again. The Magician screams with rage and there is a thud to indicate the rock falling over the entrance to the cave. The shaft of light disappears. Aladdin tries to lift the rock in vain.)

I can't even budge it. *(Pause.)* Let me out, sir. Please let me out.

I'll throw away the fruit. I'll reach you the lamp, sir. Magician—
Magician! Let me out! Please let me out! Ohhh! Magician—
*(He falls onto the step, his head buried in his arms, and sobs audibly.
He lifts his head, still sobbing.)*
I won't cry. I won't. I'll get out somehow. I will! I will!! I will!!!
*(He runs up the steps, puffing and trying very hard not to cry. He tries
again and again to lift the stone, to no avail. He comes down the
steps a little.)*
I can't get out. I'll never get out now. Even if he wanted to let me
out he couldn't lift the rock. I wish I'd reached the lamp to him.
(He suddenly starts to call in a mournful, hollow voice:) Mother!!
Mother-r-r-r — Hello-o-o—! My mother might hear me. She could
get a lot of people and they could lift the rock. Hello—Hello-o-o-o!
*(His voice trails off into a sob. He kneels down and assumes an atti-
tude of prayer.)*
Please, Allah—help me to get out of this cave. Please help me. I
don't want to stay down here all alone.
*(He begins to twist his hands in anguish. He falls on his arms and
wrings his hands in a circular motion. His face is hidden. The Genie
of the Ring appears and the slaves of the Ring are with him. The
slaves kneel in a semi-circle around Aladdin. As the Genie appears,
the stage goes into semi-darkness. Aladdin lifts his head and sees
them. He leaps up in terror.)*
Let me alone! Let me alone!
(He runs up the steps.)
GENIE: What wouldst thou?
ALADDIN: I'll put back the fruit and the lamp. The Magician told
me it was all right to take them.
GENIE: I am ready to obey thee as thy slave. I and the other slaves
of the ring.
ALADDIN: The ring? Is this the ring you mean?
(They all bow low.)
GENIE: What wouldst thou? We are thy slaves and slaves of all who
wear the ring.
ALADDIN: Does the ring belong to you?
GENIE: We belong to the ring.
ALADDIN: Take it then. The Magician told me I could wear it.
GENIE: Keep it always. You will need it again.
ALADDIN: Oh, thank you.
GENIE: Just now you turned the ring around and around without
knowing it. That is how you called us. Remember that and we will
always obey your commands.
ALADDIN: Do you want the lamp back? Shall I put it back in that
niche?
GENIE: The lamp will make your every wish come true. Never let it
out of your possession.

ALADDIN: Then what the Magician said was true! What must I do to make the lamp give me the things I wish for?

GENIE: That I am forbidden to tell you. You must find out for yourself.

ALADDIN: I did find out about turning the ring.

GENIE: Turn it and command us. What wouldst thou have?

ALADDIN: Can you help me get out of this cave?

GENIE: We can do what you command.

(The slaves start moving slowly in a circle.)

ALADDIN: Please—I want to get out of this cave. *(Pause.)* What good is a wonderful lamp to me if I am locked in this terrible cave the rest of my life?

GENIE: That is not a command.

ALADDIN: Must I command you as the Sultan commands his people?

GENIE: We cannot help you unless you do.

ALADDIN: I have never commanded anybody . . .

GENIE: If you have no tasks for us to perform, we shall leave you. Farewell!

SLAVES: Farewell! *(They start to disappear.)*

ALADDIN: No! No! Please don't go away! *(They continue to go.)* Stop! Stop! I command you to stop! . . . *(They stop. With great authority:)* I command you to help me out of this cave!

(The slaves form a circle as before. The Genie disappears. The stage begins to get dark. There is an eerie sound of wind. The slaves chant their ritual softly under the following—"Sovereign Guide," etc.)

Ohhhh—why is it getting dark? How can I see where to go? *(Wind sound.)* I wish I were on top of the ground again . . .

(There is another strong blast of wind which sounds like a siren. The stage goes completely black. There is a luminous circle where the slaves were. This is formed by luminous paint on the sleeves of their costumes. The lamp which Aladdin was holding in his hands is luminous also. There is complete silence as the luminous lamp begins slowly to ascend the steps. It goes to the top and disappears upward. As the lamp goes through the entrance to the cave, Aladdin laughs. A shaft of bright sunlight shines through the entrance, revealing the slaves in picture. In the distance is heard the faint crowing of Aladdin as the curtain falls.)

CURTAIN

ACT TWO

SCENE 1: *The scene is the same as the first scene of Act One but it is now dusk. The exterior of the cave is the same as it was before it was opened. Aladdin is lying on the ground in a sleeping posture. He is holding the lamp in one arm and still has some of the fruit from the cave. He crows softly in his sleep.*

MOTHER *(entering right as in the first act)* Aladdin!! Aladdin!!!!
   Oh, my boy, my boy! Why don't you come home to your mother?
   Aladdin—!
   (She is about to leave in despair.)
ALADDIN *(opening his eyes and looking around)*: Mother—here I am!
   (He yawns.)
MOTHER *(rushing to him)*: Oh, my boy. There you are at last! I
   have searched the whole city for you and gave up all hope of ever
   seeing you again. Where have you been?
ALADDIN: I have been having a strange dream.
MOTHER: You ought to be ashamed of yourself, worrying your poor
   old mother like this. We have nothing to eat in the house and I'm
   so tired I can work no more. We shall starve for certain.
ALADDIN: I don't remember getting sleepy. How long have I been
   gone, mother? It all seems so strange.
MOTHER: You have been gone since early morn and it is almost nightfall. What is that you have in your blouse, Aladdin? You're stuffed
   full of something.
ALADDIN *(looking at his stuffed blouse in wonder)*: It wasn't a dream
   after all.
MOTHER: I declare I never knew such a boy. It's impossible to keep
   you looking like anything. How many times do I have to tell you
   not to keep stuffing things into your blouse?
ALADDIN *(displaying fruits)*: Look how pretty they are!
MOTHER: Aladdin, where have you been?
ALADDIN: I've been in a cave, mother. A magic cave.
MOTHER: Don't talk like that. There's no such thing as magic. Don't
   let anyone hear you say such things. They'll think you've lost your
   mind. You probably need something to eat. Come along home.
ALADDIN: Look, mother. Here is the Lamp I went into the cave to
   get. It will make your every wish come true.
MOTHER: You'd better stop wishing and help your mother figure out
   a way to get something to eat.
ALADDIN: I wish I knew how to make it work. He said I had to find
   out for myself.
MOTHER: Give it to me, son. We shall take it and sell it and get a
   little money for food.

21

(She takes the lamp from Aladdin's hand.)

ALADDIN: No, mother, NO!! We mustn't sell it We mustn't. The Magician never would have gone to so much trouble to get it, if it were just an ordinary lamp. It's magic.

MOTHER: Be quiet, child. Nobody believes in magic.

ALADDIN: Give it back to me, mother. I'll find out how to work it.

MOTHER: You have caused me enough trouble already with your wild talk and deeds. It's a very dirty lamp. If you clean it up a bit, perhaps it will bring a little more money.

(She takes a cloth from her dress, rubs it in the sand and starts to polish the Lamp. Immediately, with a clash of cymbals and a puff of smoke, a tremendous Genie appears. He speaks in a thunderous voice.)

GENIE: What wouldst thou have? I am ready to obey thee as thy slave, and the slave of all those who have the Lamp in their hands.

(At his appearance and voice, the mother screams and faints. Aladdin makes a grab for the lamp, gets it from her, and rubs it.)

ALADDIN: We are hungry. Bring us something to eat.

(The slaves of the lamp enter with a table piled with rich food and gold and silver plates, or, if preferred, each with a tray. The Genie disappears, but the slaves remain, kneeling, with their hands up.)

(Aladdin fans his mother): It's all right, Mother. You mustn't be afraid.

MOTHER *(slowly coming to)*: Oh, mustn't I? You get me away from this place at once. That thing frightened me so, my teeth almost jumped right out of my mouth. Let's go home. I'm as weak as a rag.

ALADDIN: You just need something to eat, Mother. Look.

MOTHER: Goodness, son, what's all this?

ALADDIN: Food, Mother, food.

MOTHER: I can see that, child, but whose is it?

ALADDIN: Ours, mother. Help yourself.

MOTHER: Child, who sent us this great plenty? Has the Sultan heard of our great poverty, and had pity on us?

ALADDIN: That doesn't matter, Mother. It's ours. Sit down and eat.

MOTHER: No, no, I won't eat here. Let's get away from this place.

ALADDIN: Then take the food home with you.

MOTHER: We could never do that.

ALADDIN: The slaves will do your bidding, mother. I will have them carry it for you.

(There is the sound of a rooster crowing offstage. Aladdin looks eagerly toward the sound, and moves toward it. He crows in answer.)

I will remain here, mother. You will wish to go home. Slaves, transport this food to my house.

(Aladdin crows again.)

MOTHER: Why do you make that funny noise?

(Aladdin takes a large golden platter. On it he piles his wonderful fruits.)

Come, Aladdin, come home with me.

(She casts an anxious eye toward the slaves who are disappearing with

the food. She is torn between her desire not to let them out of her sight, and her anxiety over Aladdin. She seesaws between the two.)

ALADDIN: Hurry, mother.

MOTHER: Come along home, Aladdin. Oh—not so fast—wait for me— Now you hurry on home, Aladdin—Oh dear . . .

(She hurries off after the slaves. As soon as they are out of sight, Aladdin stands on the rock and crows. Adora answers him far away. Aladdin giggles excitedly and does a little jig ending in a turn that is almost a pirouette, his arms outflung. A thought comes to him, and he makes a dive for the lamp. He rubs it hastily. The Genie of the Lamp appears.)

GENIE: What wouldst thou have, young son of the earth? Command me.

ALADDIN: Could you build me a palace more beautiful than the Sultan's?

GENIE: I can fulfill your every wish.

ALADDIN: Then build it, please. And hurry. It's for the princess, and she's on her way here. She needs a palace of her very own. The Sultan's is too large for her. She gets lost in it. Make it a little palace, please, and very beautiful, and not so lonely.

GENIE: Be still, my son, and be not afraid.

ALADDIN: I'm not afraid, sir. It is my mother who gets afraid. Oh— and bring me garments befitting such a castle.

(The lights dim to a blackout. In the darkness the slaves of the lamp appear. They are dressed in phosphorescent costumes of fragile beauty. They move in a pattern which suggests the building of a castle. When they have finished, the lights come up, revealing a gossamer castle in the background, very soap-bubbly. The Genie and the slaves are gone. Aladdin in his new garments, laughs): Oo-o-o-o-oh, how beautiful. No one could ask for a more wonderful little palace. Adora will certainly be very pleased with it. I wish mother would believe in my lamp and not want to sell it. I'll have to hide it from her till she gets used to it.

ADORA *(offstage)*: Aladdin!

ALADDIN: Here I am, Adora. Hurry, hurry.

ADORA *(entering)*: Where have you been? You said you'd wait for me here, but you didn't. I had a terrible time getting away, and then when I got here, there was no one here.

ALADDIN: I've been on a wonderful journey, Adora.

ADORA: I think you might have waited for me. You said you'd take me with you.

ALADDIN: You couldn't have gone with me.

ADORA: Then I don't see why you said you'd wait for me.

ALADDIN: Don't be mad at me, Adora. If you'll stop being mad at me for a minute, I have something wonderful to show you.

ADORA: What is it?

ALADDIN: Have you stopped being mad?

ADORA: Well, yes, but I don't see why you—

23

ALADDIN: I won't show you till you've stopped being mad the least little bit.

ADORA: Show me what it is. *(Pause.)* I'm not mad any more. Really. Show me.

(They look at each other and she giggles. He giggles also.)

ALADDIN: Close your eyes. Now turn around three times.

ADORA *(as she turns)*:   I'm getting dizzy.

ALADDIN *(as he turns her around three times)*:   Around and around and around and around—now, open your eyes.

ADORA: O-o-o-o-oh—what's that?

ALADDIN: Can't you tell what it is?

ADORA: It looks like a—like a—little palace!

ALADDIN: It is a palace. It's your palace.

ADORA: But I haven't any palace of my own.

ALADDIN: Oh, yes, you have. I just gave you one.

ADORA: But it wasn't even there, this morning. How could you?

ALADDIN: Do you like it?

ADORA: Oh, yes. Where did it come from?

ALADDIN: It's a secret. Now, aren't you glad I went on my journey?

ADORA: Oh, it's wonderful. It's such a little palace. Just the kind I've always wanted. Is it really mine, for my very own?

ALADDIN: It's all yours.

ADORA: It's just the kind of palace I've always imagined. Thank you.

ALADDIN *(as she starts to cry)*:   Well, if you like it, what are you crying for?

ADORA: Something terrible has happened.

ALADDIN: What is it, Adora?

(Distant cheering begins to be heard and the noise of a great crowd approaching.)

ADORA *(sobbing)*:   I'm being bethrothed today to the son of the Grand Vizier. I'll have to live in his big palace all the time.

ALADDIN: Oh! People say the son of the Grand Vizier is a very ugly man.

ADORA: I can't help that, can I?

ALADDIN: I've also heard that he is very cross.

ADORA: Stop saying those things, Aladdin. I don't want to marry him.

ALADDIN: Then why are you being betrothed?

ADORA: My father is making me. He says I run away too much, and he thinks the son of the Grand Vizier can make me stay at home. I'd rather die than stay at home with him.

ALADDIN: Why doesn't your father let you choose a husband for yourself? You're much too young to be betrothed to anyone yet.

ADORA: The son of the Grand Vizier is very rich and he has given my father many beautiful presents. That pleases my father very much. He thinks I need great wealth to make me happy, but I don't. I'd rather live in a tailor shop than marry that silly man.

ALADDIN (*with great dignity*): There are many places worse than a tailor's shop.

ADORA: Oh, yes. A lonely palace is much worse.

ALADDIN (*after a long pause*): Where's your father?

ADORA: He went to the home of the Grand Vizier to draw up the papers for the betrothal.

(*The distant cheering comes much closer. Adora turns to look toward the noise and bursts into fresh sobs.*)

And now—here he comes!

ALADDIN: Are they shouting about the betrothal?

ADORA: Yes. It's the people of the city, cheering for my father. They're happy because of the betrothal of the Princess. They think it's a time to rejoice. Oh-h-h—I wish I were dead.

ALADDIN: Don't cry, Adora. Listen to me.

ADORA: I must go now, Aladdin. My father is almost here. He will be angry that I am not at home. I shall always remember you, as long as I live. Good-bye, Aladdin. Good-bye.

(*She starts off.*)

ALADDIN: Adora. Wait. Don't go away. (*His face suddenly brightens.*) I have a plan.

ADORA: They're getting nearer. He'll see me, Aladdin. I must go.

ALADDIN: Wait and see. I'm going to fix things, Adora.

ADORA: How can you?

ALADDIN: Didn't I get your palace for you? Isn't it what you wanted?

ADORA: You know it is.

ALADDIN: Then wait and see your father. I have something to say to him.

ADORA: I'm frightened, Aladdin. You mustn't be bold with father. He might put you in prison, and he'll be very angry with me.

ALADDIN: I promise not to make him angry. Will you wait with me?

ADORA: I'm afraid.

ALADDIN: Hide. Don't let your father see you.

(*The crowd has evidently turned a corner, for suddenly they are much louder.*)

CROWD: Hail the Sultan! Hail the Sultan! Hail—Hail—

(*As the first members of the crowd come on stage, Adora hides behind the rock. The Sultan enters under a canopy carried by slave women. He is bowing to the roaring crowd with smug condescension, first to one side, then to the other. The procession reaches center stage, and turns coming downstage, directly toward the audience. Aladdin, in the meantime, has climbed to the top of the rock where he has picked up the platter of gold and silver fruits. He carries them downstage, and interrupts the progress of the Sultan. Back to the audience, feet apart, he holds the platter of fruit in one hand, and raises the other in a gesture of command.*)

ALADDIN: Hail the Sultan!

CROWD: Out of the way, rascal—let the Sultan pass— He dares to

stand in the way of the Sultan— Out of the way—out of the way, etc.
(A group of people start to take hold of Aladdin and push him out of the way. He holds up the platter of fruit so that the Sultan can see it. The Sultan peers at it over his nose, then lifts a hand to wave away the members of the crowd who threaten Aladdin.)

SULTAN: Stop! Leave him alone. He has a gift for the Sultan. Let him advance.

(The people who are around Aladdin fall back. Aladdin advances to the Sultan, and kneels, lifting the fruit.)

CROWD: A present for the Sultan— It's a wonder his Majesty didn't have him flogged— He's a very handsome young ruffian— What beautiful clothes he wears . . . I wonder where he got them— That's Aladdin, the son of the tailor— How does he dare . . . The Sultan loves beautiful things— *(etc.)*

ALADDIN: My lord Sultan, I am greatly honored that your Majesty accepts this gift from me. I know the greatness of your power, and how much my birth is below the spendour and luster of your high rank.

SULTAN:Never in my life have I seen such unusual fruits and jewels. *(He takes the platter.)* Arise, my son. I commend you. I accept this gift with great pleasure. It pleases my magnificence to reward you with a gift in return. What would you like?

ALADDIN: You have made me very happy, your Majesty. There is only one thing in the whole world that I want.

SULTAN: Ask for it, my son. It is in my power to give you anything you wish.

ALADDIN: Then—give me the hand of your daughter, the Princess Badroulbadour.

(There is an immediate and electric silence on stage. The crowd holds its breath to see how the Sultan will take this effrontery. For a moment the royal brow is clouded in a frown. The crowd stares at Aladdin with pity for the doomed. Then the Sultan relaxes and peals of laughter issue from him. Each peal is echoed by the crowd, the whole growing into a crescendo of sound, and everyone on the stage, except Aladdin, is rocking and wiping their eyes. During this, Adora peeps out from behind the rock, stamping her foot with rage at this ridicule of Aladdin.)

SULTAN *(when he is laughed out)*: Oh—ho—heee . . . I'm afraid you would find my daughter too much of a problem, my son.

CROWD: Did you ever hear of such a thing? The Sultan has a great deal of patience— It's a good thing the Sultan is in a laughing mood today— *(etc.)*

SULTAN: Ho-ho—Oh-ho—It would take a king's ransom to satisfy her extravagant wants.

ALADDIN: I know that, sir. She must have rich presents. And I have made provision for them.

(Adora peeks out from behind the rock again and make a face.)

Your Majesty, it will be the greatest honour to me if you will accept in the name of your daughter this palace which I have had especially built for her.

(Aladdin waves a careless hand toward the palace. The crowd, following his gesture, turns and sees it. Exclamations of awe and wonder from the crowd.)

CROWD: Oh— It is a palace— Where did it come from? It wasn't there yesterday— It's beautiful— Look how it shines— It must be made of gold—Wherever did he get the money—The walls are made of diamond and crystal— The windows have lattices enriched with jewels—amethysts, rubies, emeralds—

SULTAN: By all the devils and all the gods, it is a fine palace. Where did you get it?

ALADDIN: I had it built, sir.

SULTAN: You have built a palace more beautiful than the Sultan's. How dare you!

ALADDIN: The Sultan's is much larger.

SULTAN *(calming down)*: True—true, my son. My palace is a much bigger palace.

ALADDIN: But your majesty, this palace is plenty big enough for two.

SULTAN: Only today, I have given the hand of my daughter to the son of the Grand Vizier. I have the documents with me now. All the city is rejoicing.

ALADDIN: Is a sealed document more powerful than the Sultan, your Majesty?

SULTAN: Nothing is more powerful than the Sultan! Nothing or no one. I could tear up this document and throw it in the face of the Grand Vizier if I chose But he is very rich

ALADDIN: Has he a palace for the Princess?

SULTAN: My daughter would not like me to end her bethrothal on the day it was made public. She is too proud.

ALADDIN: The Princess is as proud as she is beautiful. But if she should consent to having her bethrothal to the son of the Grand Vizier done away with, would the Sultan allow it?

SULTAN: My daughter nearly always has her own way in the end.

(Aladdin bows his way from the Sultan to the end of the rock where Adora is. He stands up very straight and reaches out one hand to Adora. She comes out from behind the rock and takes Aladdin's hand. He ushers her into the presence of the Sultan.)

ALADDIN: Her Royal Highness, the Princess Badroulbadour.

CROWD: Hail the Princess. Long live the Princess.

SULTAN: Where have you been?

ADORA: Forgive me, father. I was too unhappy to remain quietly in the palace.

SULTAN: You could never remain quietly anywhere. *(The crowd laughs. Sultan booming:)* SILENCE! How dare you laugh at the great Princess. On your knees, all of you.

27

(Their laughter dies away and they all kneel. Aladdin also kneels.)

ADORA: You have made me very happy, father.

SULTAN: How have I made you happy?

ADORA: I never wanted to be betrothed to the son of the Grand Vizier. I am too young to be betrothed.

SULTAN: You're old enough to be a great worry to me. You're old enough to go roaming about the city alone, as soon as my back is turned. You're old enough—

ADORA: But father, I . . .

SULTAN: QUIET: Not another word from you. This time I am going to punish you.

ADORA *(quietly)*: Yes, father.

SULTAN: You're too young to be betrothed, are you?

ADORA: Yes, father.

SULTAN: QUIET! I'll teach you to disobey me. Your betrothal to the son of the Grand Vizier is hereby cancelled.

(He tears up the document. There is a reaction from the crowd.)

BUT!! Too young to be betrothed, are you? I'll teach you. This time you'll do my bidding and you won't have a chance to talk yourself out of it. Arise, all of you. The Sultan hereby publicly announces the betrothal of the Princess to this young man who kneels before me.

CROWD: Hail the Sultan—

ADORA: Oh, father—

SULTAN: Not a word from you. It's all settled. This young man is younger and handsomer than the son of the Grand Vizier, and seems to have greater wealth. He will be able to keep you at home. Too young to be betrothed. Advance, young man. What is your name?

ALADDIN: My name is Aladdin, most high Sultan.

SULTAN: Advance, my daughter. What is your name? *(Adora looks at him, surprised.)* WHAT IS YOUR NAME?

ADORA: I am the Princess Badrouldabour, but my father calls me Adora.

(The crowd is amused, but the Sultan glares them into silence.)

SULTAN *(to Aladdin)*: It is with great pleasure that I confer on you the title of Prince. Prince Aladdin, it pleases the great and high Sultan to bestow upon you the hand of his daughter, the Princess Badroulbadour. You are now betrothed. My good people, your Princess is now betrothed.

CROWD: Hail to the Prince! Hail to the Princess!

(Adora bows to the people and turns back to the Sultan.)

ALADDIN: It is a great honor you have conferred upon me, your highness. I shall do all in my power to make myself worthy.

ADORA: Now, may I go to see my beautiful little palace? I can't wait to see the inside of it.

SULTAN: What does Prince Aladdin say?

ALADDIN: I shall be greatly honored to escort the Princess to her new palace.

ADORA: Let's go at once.

28

SULTAN: For myself, I shall be off to my own palace. Slaves—advance.

ADORA: Good-bye, father.

ALADDIN (bowing): Great Sultan!

(Exit, followed by the crowd, cheering.)

NOONA: Does the Princess wish me to accompany her to the little palace?

ADORA: You lead the way, Noona. We will follow.

(Exit Noona.)

ALADDIN (detainnig the Princess): Adora!

(The Magician enters, lurking in the shadows, and spies the lamp, lying carelessly on top of the great rock. He begins to creep furtively toward the lamp, with itching fingers, but his progress is slow, as he must stay out of sight.)

ADORA: I am grateful to you for saving me from the son of the Grand Vizier.

ALADDIN: But you are still betrothed, and you said you were too young to be betrothed. Would you like me to go somewhere very far away?

ADORA (coyly): I am glad to be betrothed to you, Prince. (He approaches her with a bound. She giggles.) You are the funniest prince I have ever met.

ALADDIN: I can stand on my head, and do backward somersaults. Would you like me to?

ADORA: What fun it will be! (She becomes a grand lady for a minute.) The Princess holds court today. Will the Prince kindly get down off his head? The guests are coming.

ALADDIN (laughing): I shall stand on my head only when there are no guests.

ADORA: Come, let's go to the little palace.

ALADDIN: At your service, Princess.

(He makes a courtly bow, and starts out with her ceremoniously. The Magician is delighted, and taking a long stride, begins to reach for the lamp. But Aladdin remembers the lamp, just in time, and makes a sudden short stop.)

Oh, I nearly forgot!

(He runs quickly up the rock, to get the lamp. The Magician, who almost has the lamp in his grasp, is forced to hide. Aladdin takes the lamp to Adora.)

Would you mind keeping this lamp for me, in the little palace? I dare not take it home. My mother wants to sell it.

ADORA: It's a funny old lamp, isn't it? It's quite dirty.

(As she takes it from him, the lights start to dim.)

ALADDIN: Yes, but it is very valuable to me. Will you keep it safe for me—until the wedding?

ADORA (swinging it carelessly): Of course, Aladdin. Now come along. It's getting dark.

(There is a burst of music and cheering heard offstage.)

ALADDIN (turning toward it): Listen!

ADORA (listens, then giggles): The people are happy about us.

29

ALADDIN: So am I.

(They crow together very softly, then turn to look at the palace. In the dusky light, it gleams with new splendor.)

Oh, it's beautiful . . . it's beautiful . . . it's *beautiful!* Come, Aladdin!

(They leave the stage in high spirits. Music and cheering are heard offstage. The Magician is left glowering. He shakes his fist after the two children.)

MAGICIAN: Keep the lamp for him until the wedding! Heh, heh, heh! That lamp will be in my hands before there is any wedding, *Prince* Aladdin!

(He laughs in his evil way. The castle glows for a moment in the darkness. From one side of the stage Aladdin and the Princess are heard crowing in the distance. From the other side comes the sinister laugh of the Magician.)

CURTAIN

ACT TWO

SCENE 2: *When the curtain rises the stage is in darkness. The slaves of the lamp are present, but not visible, since their costumes are phosphorescent only on the front. As each slave speaks, he turns, so that the costumes produce glowing designs in the dark. Aladdin crosses the stage, and stops to wave toward the little palace. He crows, offstage, at a distance. The Princess crows back. Aladdin goes off.*

FIRST SLAVE: Two children of the earth are happy tonight.

SECOND: Tonight, but not tomorrow.

(Magician's laugh is heard offstage.)

THIRD: There is danger in the air tonight.

FOURTH: The danger of approaching evil.

FIRST: Evil thoughts travel fast.

SECOND: Evil men travel fast.

(Pause, Drum beat, off.)

THIRD: An evil man draws near.

FOURTH: He knows where our master, the lamp, is residing.

FIRST: He knows the secret of the desert sand.

SECOND: And the stars that hang in the sky at night.

THIRD: He casts the points of the Universe.

FOURTH: He foretells the passing of present events.

(Echoes offstage.)

FIRST: He knows our master, the lamp, is in the hands of the little Princess.

SECOND: He knows Aladdin is not by her side.

THIRD: He knows.

FOURTH: He knows.

FIRST: Will he take our master, the lamp, away from the little Princess?

SECOND: He cannot take it away from her.

THIRD: The Princess would never let him have it.

ALL: He is sly. He is cunning.

FOURTH: He can procure the lamp by trickery.

FIRST: The people of the earth are easily deceived.

SECOND: Will he deceive the little Princess?

FOURTH: We can read it in the air when it happens, but not before.

SECOND: The Princess would never let him have it.

THIRD: Wait and see.

FOURTH: Wait and see.

FIRST: The Magician draws near.

ALL: The slaves of the Lamp depart.

(They all turn their backs to the audience, thus seeming to disappear. They clear stage, unseen.)

31

MAGICIAN (offstage): New lamps for old—new lamps—shiny new lamps for old!!! New lamps—new lamps for old. New lamps for old . . .
(He enters with a stick over his shoulder, with new lamps hanging from each end. He carries a lighted lamp in one hand. The stage becomes light enough to see, with the light concentrated in the center. It is full of sinister shadows as he turns toward the palace, cups his hands and shouts louder than ever:)
New lamps—new lamps for old—silver lamps—gold lamps—crystal lamps. Lamps for a crystal palace—new lamps for old!

KALISSA *(running on)*: Here are lamps. Old lamps. Let me see the ones you have. I want the best of them.

MAGICIAN: Here they are. Massy gold and silver, and jeweled and carven jade.

KALISSA: This is the one I want.

MAGICIAN: No, no, no, no. Not that one.

KALISSA: Why not?

MAGICIAN: This one is for the Princess' little palace. Any other you may have.

KALISSA: Why do you carry a lamp for the Palace?

MAGICIAN: I give away new lamps for old so that people may learn how fine are the wares I carry. If there is one of my lamps in the Palace, everyone will wish to trade with me. Now I'll tell you what I'll do. If you will get someone from the palace to trade an old lamp for this one, I will give you all the new lamps I have left.

KALISSA: I am soft of foot and quick of finger. Perhaps I could get an old lamp from the Palace, myself. But I think you're jesting. It's mean of you to do so.

MAGICIAN: My good woman, I was never more serious in my life.

KALISSA: Oh, then sir, I shall go. I shall go at once—

MAGICIAN: Find the handmaiden of the Princess. Tell her I have a beautiful lamp of the finest crystal, especially made for the Princess. All she must do to procure it, is bring me an old lamp from the Palace to trade for it. She will jump at the opportunity.

KALISSA: You will truly give me all those others if I do?

MAGICIAN: I will give you all I have left when you return with her. You'd better hurry and get back before I sell more.

KALISSA: I go at once.
(She exits runing. The Magician chuckles to himself. Aladdin's mother enters.)

MOTHER: Was it you who cried new lamps for old?

MAGICIAN: It was indeed, my good woman. Have you old lamps to trade?

MOTHER: Well, yes, I have one. But I don't have it with me. If I pick a new one out, will you save it for me till I go home and get an old one? You see, it belongs to my son. He must be home with it by now.

32

MAGICIAN: Oh, you say your son has a lamp?

MOTHER: Oh, yes. It's very old and quite dirty, but he doesn't want to sell it for some reason, although goodness knows why.

MAGICIAN: People can get attached to small things for strange reasons. Would you mind telling me your son's name, good woman?

MOTHER: Oh, no, I'm very proud of my son. Only today he was made a Prince by the Sultan. He is now called Prince Aladdin.

MAGICIAN: Oh, yes. I have heard of him, myself. Would you recognize your son's lamp if you saw it?

MOTHER: Oh, yes indeed. I had it in my hands only today.

MAGICIAN (knowingly): Ohhh—I'll tell you what I will do for you. Since your son is a fine Prince, I will trust you with a new lamp before you bring me the old one. This is a carven lamp from India. Take it home with my blessing.

MOTHER: Oh, you are very kind, sir.

MAGICIAN: Take it at once, good woman, and go. If you cannot find the old lamp, don't bother to return this one. I will come to see you tomorrow at your tailor shop.

MOTHER: I promise, sir. But how did you know that I lived there?

MAGICIAN (bowing her off): I told you I had heard of your son. Now good evening to you.

MOTHER: I never got anything for nothing before. It doesn't seem right.

MAGICIAN (getting rid of her): Here. Take the lamp. I see another customer.

MOTHER: Oh, thank you, sir. And may Allah bless you.

MAGICIAN (almost pushing her off): Good evening, Madam.

MOTHER: This will make Aladdin happy.
(She hurries off. The Magician stands and laughs after her.)

MAGICIAN (to himself): What an escape!
(He chuckles as Kalissa and Noona appear. The Magician turns his back to them, scarcely able to control his excitement when he sees the lamp in Noona's hands.)

KALISSA: Here it is, sir.

NOONA: It's a very old and dirty lamp. Are you willing to take it?

MAGICIAN: Certainly, my child. I shall be pleased to have one of my lamps in the Palace of the little Princess.

NOONA: But it doesn't seem quiet honest. Such an old lamp. I'm not sure that the Princess would like me to.

MAGICIAN (holding up new lamp): Think how beautiful this will be in the Palace.

KALISSA: I'm sure she will like it. You will gain great favor with her.

NOONA: Ohhh—It is beautiful. (She hestitates a moment, then:) Here—take the old one. (She holds on to the old one a moment longer.) I do hope I am doing the right thing.
(The Magician keeps holding the new lamp in front of her, almost beside himself.)

Thank you, kind lady, for telling me about such a beautiful lamp.

KALISSA: I'm always glad to do anyone a favor.

NOONA *(to Magician)*: Here. Give me the new one. *(They exchange.)*

MAGICIAN: With pleasure, my child.

NOONA: Oh, thank you. I shall take it straight away to the Palace.
(She starts to go. The Magician cannot restrain a chuckle. Noona turns back.)
Why do you laugh like that, sir?

MAGICIAN: It pleases me to think of the pleasure I have given to the little Princess.
(Noona exits toward the Palace. Magician turns to Kalissa.)
Here. Take them. Take all of them. I give them to you gladly.

KALISSA: Yes—yes! Thank you, old man. I think you must be crazy.
(She hurries offstage with the lamps.)

MAGICIAN *(alone with lamp)*: At last I have you. At last. I'll never let you out of my hands again. I'll teach that young rascal to defy me. A little Palace for the Princess——indeed!!!! *(To lamp:)* We have work to do— *(Laughs.)*
(He rubs the lamp vigorously. Cymbals and smoke. The Genie of the Lamp appears. The Magician's lamp is simultaneously extinguished. Muffled drums.)

GENIE: What wouldst thou? I am ready to obey thee as thy slave. I and the other slaves of the Lamp.

MAGICIAN: Remove the Palace of the Princess. Transport it to my home in Africa. Leave no trace of it.

GENIE: I must obey.

MAGICIAN: Carry it to Africa with the Princess in it. Carry me there also. I have more work for you there when we arrive.

GENIE: Your will must be our will. It shall be done.
(His movements begin the magic and the lights lower. There is a sound of muffled drums offstage. They are low and resounding but rhythmic. The slaves gather in formation and move to the beat of the drum. There is the sound of wind, thin and shrill. The slaves do a dance with their lines of light pointing to the Palace. It starts to move off. The slaves in a mass move in the same direction, their arms of pulsing light urging the Palace on its journey. The Palace and slaves disappear. Aladdin's crow is heard off, then his voice singing. He is singing to the rising moon which floods the stage with a cold blue light. The Magician has cleared stage for the dance of the slaves. His laugh is heard off as the Palace starts to move. When the Palace is gone, Kalissa appears, crossing the stage to show off her newly acquired lamps. She stops short, as she sees the Palace is missing.)

KALISSA: Merciful Allah! The Palace! It's gone! It's gone! Sultan! Oh, great Sultan! *(She runs off, calling for the Sultan at the top of her voice.)*

ALADDIN *(heard just offstage)*: The moon is rising in the sky,
I saw him wink his other eye.
He makes a light as bright as day.
For me to see to find my way.

(He laughs aloud.)
I feel as though I could jump over the tallest tree! Wheeee!!!
(He bounds onto the stage, and starts across at top speed. He suddenly stops dead. His laughter freezes. He stands stunned.)
This is the place. I'm sure it's the place.
(He looks right and left, runing back and forth.)
I must have lost my way.
(He bounds to the top of the rock.)
It's gone. My Palace is gone— *(weakly)* Adora! Adora!
(As a last hope he crows mournfully. There is no answer. In the distance the voice of a crowd starts, menacing. His mother runs on.)
MOTHER: Aladdin! Where are you!!!
ALADDIN: What's that noise?
MOTHER: Run, my son. And pray for deliverance!
ALADDIN: What's the matter? Why do the people shout so?

(Kalissa enters.)
MOTHER: They're crying for vengeance! The Sultan is leading them.
KALLISSA: They're looking for an evil Prince who was betrothed to the Princess.
ALADDIN: I am that Prince, and I am not evil. Why do they say that?
MOTHER: They will tear you to pieces.
ALADDIN: I'm not afraid. I've done no wrong.
KALISSA *(calling off)*: Here he is. Here is the evil Prince!
CROWD *(off)*: Down with him!
MOTHER: Run, Aladdin! Run!
ALADDIN: I will not run. I am not evil!
CROWD *(rushing on stage)*: There he is! Down with him! There he is!
(Ad lib. from crowd.) The Sultan—make way for the Sultan!
SULTAN *(entering through crowd)*: Where is my daughter?
ALADDIN: I don't know, sir, but I—
SULTAN: What have you done with her?
ALADDIN: I came here to see her and found the Palace gone.
NOONA: My mistress has vanished and you are to blame.
ALADDIN: Why are you not with the Princess?
NOONA: I came here to fix a surprise for her, and before I got back the Palace was gone.
SULTAN: You shall pay for this with your life. Put him in chains!
ALADDIN: I would not harm the Princess. You ought to know that. Give me a little time and—
SULTAN: A curse on you. I've listened enough to your idle pleadings. You shall die. I wish I had never laid eyes on you. My daughter would be safe at home. Ahhhh—my little Adora, I shall never see her again . . .

35

(Aladdin suddenly remembers the ring. He holds his hand up, looking at it and laughs triumphantly. The crowd roars in fury. He lifts his hand in command. They gradually quiet down.)

ALADDIN: I will find the Princess. Give me a little time, your highness!

SULTAN: You dare to plead for mercy. *Where is my daughter?* WHERE IS SHE????

ALADDIN: I know I can find her. I can! I can! Leave me here, alone.

KALISSA: He's trying to save his skin.

ALADDIN *(holding the ring and looking at it)*:   Listen to me! I know a secret way!

(Crowd jeers and presses up to the rock.)

SULTAN: Chain him! Chain him!!!

(Two climb onto the rock. They have heavy chains which clank. They chain his arms and legs. His arms are chained in front of him.)

ALADDIN *(over the jeers and boos of the crowd)*:   All right! Put me in chains! Put me in prison if you like!

(Again he looks at the ring which is visible even though his hands are chained together.)

I'll save the Princess in spite of you! I will! I will! I will save the Princess!!!

(He lifts his chained hands above his head in triumph as the curtain falls.)

CURTAIN

ACT THREE

The Princess' room in her little palace, in Africa, a few hours later.
The room is shiny and full of windows. The Princess is lying asleep in
troubled dreams. The Magician enters stealthily, carrying a flask of wine
and two glasses. The glasses are of different colours. He stops to look
down at the sleeping Princess, then starts for the table.

ADORA *(in her sleep)* : Aladdin—Aladdin—
  (He stops and turns to look back at her.)
MAGICIAN: Still dreaming of Aladdin, little Princess? This wine will
  put a stop to that.
  (He continues to the table and sets down the glasses. He holds the flask
  up, peering through it.)
  There is no wine in all the world as rare as this. A thousand thousand
  years ago, this flask was sealed. The first magician put the first
  enchantment on it.
  (He breaks the seal, passes the flask back and forth, sniffing it. He laughs
  low, and pours two glassfulls. He lifts one and turns to the Princess.)
  One drink of this, Princess, will make your little heart as hard as
  mine. You will forget your fine Prince Aladdin. Even if he finds
  out how to use the ring, and comes to your rescue, you will not remember him. This wine will make you help me get back the ring from
  him—and then—leave your Prince Aladdin to me. No one must
  share the secret of the lamp with us.
  (He takes the lamp from the window ledge and puts it in his bosom.)
  She will be waking soon. *(He leaves.)*
ADORA *(coming out of her sleep)*: Aladdin—Aladdin—
  (She sits up straight, facing the audience. She brushes her hand across
  her eyes and sighs. She calls, quickly at first.)
  Noona, Noona—Noona . . . Noona— Come and sit beside me, Noona.
  I just had the most terrible dream. Noona—
  (There is no answer. Adora looks a little alarmed, then calls again in
  a commanding voice.)
  Noona!
  (She springs to her feet. She draws herself up with royal authority, and
  is about to call again, when she suddenly sees the scenery outside the
  windows. It is completely different from what she has known. She
  calls again, confused and panicky, running to the door.)
  Noona— NOONA—
  (The Magician steps through the door just as she reaches it. She backs
  up and screams.)
  Oh-h-h-h-h—
MAGICIAN: Quiet, child.

37

ADORA: Who are you?

MAGICIAN: I will not harm you if you do as I say.

ADORA: Go away. NOONA—

MAGICIAN: You needn't call for anyone. We are the only two people in the palace.

ADORA: What are you doing here? Get out of my palace.

MAGICIAN: . I have something to say to you.

ADORA: I'll call the guards and have you put out.

MAGICIAN: There are no guards, Princess.

(She starts toward the door. The Magician blocks her exit.)

ADORA: Let me pass.

MAGICIAN: Listen to what I have to tell you.

ADORA: I am the Princess Badroulbadour. Let me pass. Let me out, I tell you.

(She rushes to the door and he stops her by force.)

How dare you! FATHER!

MAGICIAN: No one will hear you, Princess. You might as well keep quiet and listen.

ADORA: I will not.

MAGICIAN: You'll have to.

ADORA: I'll jump out the window.

(She leaps onto the sill and looks out. She shrinks back in terror, then she leans forward, and she stares down, her gaze showing the great height at which the palace is placed.)

MAGICIAN: It's a high jump, Princess.

ADORA *(peering down and down)*: Oh-h-h-h— There wasn't a rocky precipice below my window. I never saw this place before. Even the stars are all different. There's a cross in the sky.

MAGICIAN: We are in a strange country. While you slept, your palace was transported to Africa.

ADORA: Africa! That's not true.

MAGICIAN: Look out the window.

ADORA *(running from one side to the other)*: Such a thing could never happen.

MAGICIAN: Your palace was built in a minute. Did you think that could ever happen?

ADORA: Yes. It did happen. Aladdin built it for me.

MAGICIAN: In a minute.

ADORA: Yes.

MAGICIAN: If Aladdin has the power to build this palace in a minute, he would have the power to move it to Africa, wouldn't he?

ADORA: Aladdin would never do that, never.

MAGICIAN: He has done it.

ADORA: Why should he?

MAGICIAN: Evil minds work in a strange fashion.

ADORA: Aladdin is not evil. I forbid you to say such a thing.

MAGICIAN: Who else could have done it, Princess?

ADORA (*almost in tears*): I don't know.

MAGICIAN: But you are here.

ADORA: Shall I never see my father again?

MAGICIAN: I hope so, child, if you do as I say.

ADORA: People do not talk like that to the Princess.

MAGICIAN: You must realize that you will be better off if you are friends with me. I am the only one who can help you.

ADORA: Then get word to my father at once and tell him where I am.

MAGICIAN: I'll get word to the Sultan as soon as possible. It takes many months to get word so far. You must be patient.

ADORA: I don't believe you. You don't want my father to know.

MAGICIAN: It is unwise of you to be rude to me.

ADORA: Why won't you let me pass that door?

MAGICIAN: I want to help you.

ADORA: Let me out of the palace, and I can find help for myself. My father is known all over the world.

MAGICIAN: No, no, Princess. I keep you here to protect you.

ADORA: That's not so. If Aladdin were here, you wouldn't keep me shut in. You'd be afraid to.

MAGICIAN: Don't you understand yet that Aladdin is to blame for your being here?

ADORA: No, I don't. Aladdin would always help me. Oh-h-h-h—

MAGICIAN: You believe me after all?

ADORA: No. (*She sits.*) I had a terrible dream. I dreamed that I was in trouble and Aladdin was trying to come and help me, but he could hardly walk because his feet were tied with chains.

MAGICIAN: Your dream was almost true, Princess. I have learned through a secret messenger that your fine Prince is lying in your father's prison. His feet are in chains, and so are his hands. He is waiting sentence for the crime of causing the disappearance of the Princess and her palace. Now, do you still believe in him?

ADORA: Go away. GO AWAY.
(*Aladdin crows in the distance. Adora stops dead. She can't believe her ears. She starts to the window, then checks herself.*)

MAGICIAN (*turning to wine he set down on entering*): Don't be such a little fool. Forget about your traitorous Aladdin.

ADORA: I shall never forget about Aladdin.

MAGICIAN: My child, I have brought you some rare old wine, the best in all Africa. Will you do me the honor of having a glass with me?

ADORA: I don't want any wine. Go away and leave me.

MAGICIAN: Very well, Princess, I will go. I shall be right down the hall. If you want me, knock on the floor three times with this stick.
(*The Magician hands her the stick, and goes to the window and locks it.*)
I will lock this window.

ADORA: No, no—
(*Aladdin crows again, a little nearer.*)

MAGICIAN: It is very high. You might fall out.

ADORA: I'll be very careful. Please leave it open.

MAGICIAN: You are safer with it locked. *(He goes to the door and takes the key from his pocket.)* I will lock this door also, to protect you from harm. *(He smiles.)* When you have grown quite tired of being locked in, call me, and I shall be glad to have a glass of this delicious wine with you. Pleasant dreams, Princess.

(He exits with a low chuckle and a sinister grin. Adora has turned her back to him. As soon as the sound of the key turning in the lock is heard, Adora is very alert. She runs to the window and tries to open it. She can't. She crows, as close to the window as possible, and waits for an answer. There is none. She is frantic. She tugs at the window again, to no avail. She crows again, loudly and mournfully. She stops and waits in despair.)

ADORA: It was Aladdin. I'm sure it was. No one else would know our signal. If the window were open, he would hear. He'll think I'm not here. *(She tugs at the window again.)* Why doesn't he crow again? What if I just imagined I heard him? He could never get into the palace, even if he were here. Maybe he thinks I'm not here, because I don't answer.

(She gives up in despair, and starts down stage, sobbing softly. She looks around the room, then stands for a bit, the picture of misery.) Oh, my little palace—are you unhappy, too, to be so far away from home?

(She sits, back to the window. She breaks down a little more. Aladdin appears outside the window. He seems to appear from nowhere. He holds up one hand and the window opens. He pulls himself in and sits on the sill.)

ALADDIN *(very softly)*: Adora . . .

(Adora looks up and straight ahead without turning. She can't believe she has heard right. She turns around slowly and when she sees him, She jumps to her feet and runs almost to him and stops. She is overcome with emotion.)

ADORA: Aladdin . . .

ALADDIN *(very casually, quite brightly, trying not to show concern)*: Hello.

ADORA: Oh, Aladdin!

ALADDIN: Are you all right, Adora?

ADORA: How did you get here?

ALADDIN: Where's the Magician?

ADORA: Who?

ALADDIN: The old man who brought you here.

ADORA: Oh-h-h-h—he said you brought me here.

ALADDIN: Oh, he did, did he?

ADORA: But I didn't believe him, Aladdin, honestly I didn't.

ALADDIN: Where is he?

ADORA: He's down the hallway.

ALADDIN: Right near?

ADORA: He's waiting for me to call him, but I won't.

ALADDIN: We must think fast, Adora. We've got to get away from here.

ADORA: We can't, Aladdin. He has me locked in. He locked me in my little palace. How did you get in through that locked window?

ALADDIN: I'll explain that later. I have a secret plan to save you. I must hide somewhere.

ADORA: This closet is covered by the curtains. No one could see you there.

ALADDIN: Oh, yes, I remember.

ADORA: Can't you tell me a little bit about your secret plan? Maybe I could help you.

ALADDIN: All right. Listen closely. See this ring? It's magic. The Genie of the ring brought me here. That's how I got up the high precipice and through the locked window.

ADORA: Is it really magic?

ALADDIN: Do you remember the lamp I gave you to keep for me?

ADORA: Noona took it to exchange it for a beautiful new one.

ALADDIN (with an undercurrent in his voice): I know she did.

ADORA: She was so happy about it, Aladdin, that I couldn't bear to—· But she never came back with the new one.

ALADDIN: The lamp is more magic. Much more magic than the ring. The lamp alone has the power to take us home. We have to get back.

ADORA: Oh—where can we find it?

ALADDIN: The old Magician has it. That's how he sent you here.

ADORA: I know where it is. He was carrying something in his blouse. It must be the lamp.

ALADDIN: Of course it is. He would never let it out of his sight.

ADORA: We'll never get it back so long as he carries it with him.

ALADDIN: See this?

ADORA: What is it?

ALADDIN: It's a magic powder. The slaves of the ring gave it to me. If we can find a way to make him take all of it, he'll go to sleep at once and sleep for a day and a night.

ADORA: I knew I could help you, Aladdin. I knew I could.

ALADDIN: What do you mean, Adora?

ADORA: I have a plan, too.

ALADDIN: You musn't put yourself in any danger, Adora.

ADORA: See this wine? The old man brought it in, just now, and asked me to drink it with him. I said I didn't want it, and he got angry and locked me in here. I'll pretend I have changed my mind and ask him to drink with me. I'll put the powder in his glass.

ALADDIN: I don't want you to be friends with him.

ADORA: I won't really be friends.

ALADDIN: Well—all right—I'll be right behind these curtains and see that no harm comes to you.

(They hurry very fast, and put the powder in one of the glasses and she pours the wine. She takes the Magician's stick.)

ADORA: Now. Hide.

ALADDIN *(behind the curtain)*: Can you see me at all, now?

ADORA: Right by the wall—now that finger shows—now your head makes a bump in the curtain. There, that's all right.

(She lifts the stick to strike the floor, then stops.)

Aladdin—

ALADDIN: What's the matter?

ADORA: Oh—nothing. I'm—I'm not afraid.

ALADDIN: Wait—

ADORA: Don't talk so loud.

ALADDIN: Be sure he drinks it all, or it might not work.

ADORA: I will.

(She strikes on the floor three times. The Magician enters after unlocking the door.)

MAGICIAN: Well, my child, I am very pleased that you have called me in. What can I do to please the little Pricess?

(Aladdin peeks out from behind the curtain, furious with him.)

ADORA: I knocked for you, sir, because I—because I—

MAGICIAN: What is it, child? Speak up.

ADORA: I've been thinking, sir. I'm sorry I was rude to you. But I was so frightened I didn't know what I was saying.

MAGICIAN: I knew you were upset, my child. I hope now that you realize that I am your friend, and will be ready to do what I ask.

ADORA: That is why I called you, sir. I have poured out the wine and will drink with you if you wish.

MAGICIAN: I'm pleased that you have decided to drink with me. I am sure you will say that you have never tasted better.

ADORA: I hope you will enjoy the taste of it, too, sir.

MAGICIAN: Of course I shall. You are a polite child, when you wish to be.

ADORA: Shall we exchange glasses? It is the custom of my country.

MAGICIAN: By all means.

ADORA *(handing him her glass)*: It's a polite custom, don't you think?

MAGICIAN: Charming, my child, charming.

(He takes her glass and reaches his to her.)

The Princess. Long may she live.

ADORA: To you, sir. May you—have pleasant dreams.

(The Magician laughs, and takes a good gulp. Adora pretends to sip hers.)

MAGICIAN: That is a pretty toast. Pleasant dreams—ha-ha-ha—

ADORA: The wine is truly delicious.

MAGICIAN: That's strange. This wine does not taste like the wine I brought you.

ADORA: It must be, sir. It's the only bottle I have. Won't you have some more, sir? If you will empty your glass, I will refill it for you.

(The Magician starts to shake his head, slight but jerky.)

ADORA *(trying to sound calm)*: Don't you feel well, sir

MAGICIAN *(seriously)*: What's in this wine?

ADORA: Mine tastes very good sir.
(He starts to get up and staggers slightly. He smells his wine.)
MAGICIAN: This wine has been poisoned.
ADORA: I feel no ill effect, sir. You must imagine it. Drink the rest of it, and perhaps you will feel better.
MAGICIAN: Why are you so anxious to have me drink the rest of it?
(He gets to his feet again, weaving unsteadily.)
I imagined it, eh? I suppose I imagine that I cannot stand straight. *(He yawns.)* I imagine that I feel a stupor coming over it. There's one thing I don't imagine—you have purposely tried to poison me.
(He picks up his glass and starts toward her.)
Here—drink the rest of this yourself.
ADORA: No!
MAGICIAN: If it is not poison, drink it. DRINK IT!
ADORA: I won't! I won't!
MAGICIAN *(yelling)*: Haaaaaaaaaaaaaa-ah— I was a fool not to suspect you. It is poison.
(He takes his glass with the remaining wine in it, and smashes it on the floor near Adora. She screams. Magician yells thickly.)
I'll throw you into the dungeon.
(He staggers toward Adora, with glazing eyes.)
ADORA: Let me alone! Let me alone!
(As he gets almost to her, Aladdin leaps from behind the curtains, and onto the Magician's back. The Magician falls backward, partly on Aladdin. Aladdin extricates himself, and stands over the Magician with clenched fists.)
ALADDIN: You will, will you?
(The Magician lets out a harrowing scream and scrambles to his feet. He lunges for Aladdin. Aladdin jumps out of his way.)
MAGICIAN: Aha—it's you. What are you doing here?
ALADDIN: I'll show you what I'm doing.
(The Magician makes another lunge for Aladdin. Aladdin pushes a chair in his way and he falls over it.)
You needn't try to hurt me, old Magician. You forget that I am protected by the magic ring you gave me.
MAGICIAN: Hah—I'll show you—
(He snatches the lamp from his blouse and attempts to rub it. Aladdin quickly jumps on him and prevents him.)
ALADDIN: No, you don't.
(They roll over and over on the floor in a frantic tussle. They roll all the way across the stage. Aladdin finally gets the lamp and yells to Adora, holding the lamp out of the reach of the Magician.)
Take it, Adora. Take it.
(Adora rushes to him and takes the lamp. Aladdin gets loose and jumps to his feet. He stands over the Magician, panting.)
How do you like the wine, old man? Why don't you drink the rest of it?

43

(The Magician gets to his feet and makes a lunge for Adora.)

MAGICIAN: Give me my lamp. Give it to me—

ADORA: I won't! I won't!

(The Magician keeps coming at her, and she starts to run. He pursues her. Just as he gets almost to her, Aladdin runs between them and takes the lamp from her.)

ALADDIN: Here it is, old Magician.

MAGICIAN *(to Aladdin)*: Put that lamp down. PUT IT DOWN!

ALADDIN: Here is your lamp. Why don't you come and get it?

MAGICIAN: I'll tear you to pieces.

ALADDIN: Try it. Just try it. Aren't you sorry you gave me this ring?

MAGICIAN: How dare you? How dare you?

(He makes a mighty lunge for Aladdin, and starts to stagger. He groans.) Oh-h-h-h-h-h-h-h! Oh-h-h-h-h-h-hhh! Everything's getting dark. Ohohohohohh—

(He gives one tremendous bellow and falls on the floor near the draped closet. He groans more softly. He tries to lift his head again, but it is too much effort, and it falls limply on his arms. He starts to breathe heavily. His sleep must be a pleasant one, for he is smiling sweetly.)

ALADDIN: *Whew!*—that was a narrow escape!

ADORA: Do you think he's really asleep?

ALADDIN *(punching him to make sure)*: I was afraid he didn't drink enough of it.

ADORA: Perhaps that's why it took him so long to go to sleep.

ALADDIN: Do you suppose he'll stay asleep as long as if he'd taken it all?

ADORA: Oh—I don't know.

ALADDIN *(listening close)*: He's very sound asleep.

ADORA: He went very suddenly. He might wake up suddenly.

ALADDIN: Let's try and see.

ADORA: Shall we?

ALADDIN: Yes. Are you afraid, Adora?

ADORA: No. I'm just excited. Touch him.

(Aladdin sets the lamp down and touches the Magician. No response. Adora blows in his face, but he only smiles serenely in his sleep. Adora, gingerly and delicately, pulls his hair.)

ALADDIN *(dragging him about)*: It would take an earthquake to wake him up.

ADORA: You can do anything you want with him. He's having pleasant dreams.

ALADDIN: What shall we do with him?

ADORA: Put him behind the curtain. I don't like to look at him. Can't we just go away and leave him?

ALADDIN: Do you want to leave your little palace in Africa?

ADORA: Oh, no, Aladdin, but what can we do? I want to see my father.

ALADDIN: The lamp can take the palace home again. Would you like that?

ADORA: It would be wonderful. Can we start right away?

ALADDIN: Oh, yes, if I give the order.

ADORA: Won't father be glad to see us?

ALADDIN: He won't be glad to see me, Adora. He'll order me put to death.

ADORA: I won't let him.

ALADDIN: You can't stop him. He thinks I stole you and the palace away. He put me in prison and proclaimed through all the streets that I should die tomorrow. When he finds out I escaped, he'll have me killed as soon as he sees me.

ADORA: No, he won't. I'll tell him it was you who saved me.

ALADDIN: He won't listen to you. I tried to talk to him. I tried to tell him I could find you. He just kept on saying, "You shall die." No one can make him listen.

ADORA: I can. I'll look at him until he smiles at me. Then I'll tell him I was carried away by magic.

ALADDIN: He won't believe you. He says there's no such thing as magic. He's like my mother. No, I don't think I'd better go near your father.

ADORA: I can't go home without you, Aladdin. I don't want to be without you any more.

ALADDIN: Do you want your father to put me to death?

ADORA: I know what to do. Your lamp moved the palace here—can't it bring my father here?

ALADDIN: Yes, if I tell it to.

ADORA: Oh—make it bring him here, Aladdin. That will make him believe in magic. We won't go home until he says he does.

ALADDIN: Yes, and we'll take the Magician home with us, and your father will put him in prison. Then when he wakes up, the people will know who was really to blame. And I know something else to do. *(He seizes the lamp.)*
Now you must promise not to be frightened, Adora.

ADORA: I won't. I promise. But let's put the curtain over the Magician before they come. I don't like to look at him.
(After they have completely concealed the Magician from sight, Aladdin takes the lamp and starts to rub it. A thought occurs to him and he hesitates.)

ALADDIN: Now watch. You may as well get used to this.
(He rubs the lamp and, with a clash of cymbals and a puff of smoke, the Genie appears.)

GENIE: What wouldst thou?

ADORA: Oh—you won't go away from me, will you, Aladdin?

ALADDIN: No, I'll stay right here. Transport to this room at once, the father of the Princess— *(He gurgles with delight at his further thought.)* Transport to this room at once—my mother.

GENIE: It shall be done.

ALADDIN: Whirl them round and round all the way. And every time they say they don't believe in magic, whirl them some more.

GENIE: It shall be done.

45

ALADDIN: As soon as they believe in magic, transport this little palace and everybody in it, back where it was built.

GENIE: It shall be done.

(The Genie dims out. Immediately there is a confused hubbub off stage. We hear the Sultan and the mother, protesting at their journey through space.)

SULTAN *(off stage)*: I command you to tell me what's happening—

MOTHER *(off)*: Oh-oh-oh-oh-ohhhh—NO!

SULTAN *(off)*: Stop me! *STOP ME!*

MOTHER *(off)*s Glubb, glubb—urggh—mlglumph—*HELP!*

SULTAN *(whirling onto the stage)*: What in the name of all that's holy—

MOTHER *(whirling on)*: Oh—oh—ohhhhh—

ADORA *(rushing to her father)*: Father—

SULTAN *(taking her in his arms)*: Adora—

MOTHER *(rushing to Aladdin)*: Aladdin—

ALADDIN *(nonchanantly)*: Hello, mother.

MOTHER: What's happening to us?

ALADDIN: We're in Africa, mother.

MOTHER: Hush up, Aladdin. Don't say such things.

SULTAN: I demand an explanation.

ADORA: You've torn your nightgown, father.

SULTAN: It was probably struck by lightning.

(He grabs a large rent in his nightgown, which reveals an expanse of royal leg. Aladdin drapes the Sultan in his own cloak.)

MOTHER: It was awful. I was brutally whisked through the top of a tall tree, and lost my best nightcap.

(Adora puts her cape around the mother.)

SULTAN: Whoever is responsible for dragging me out of bed in the middle of the night is going to suffer for it.

ADORA: It was magic, father.

SULTAN and MOTHER: There's no such thing as magic.

(They immediately begin to whirl.)

SULTAN *(to Aladdin)*: What are you doing here? Why aren't you in prison?

ALADDIN: The magic ring brought me here, sir.

SULTAN: Don't try to hoodwink me. There's no such thing as a magic ring. *(Whirls.)* Who is this woman?

ALADDIN: This is my mother, sir.

ADORA: The mother of Prince Aladdin, father.

SULTAN: He is no longer Prince. He escaped from prison. He shall die for it.

ADORA: No, father—

SULTAN: He shall die.

ALADDIN: Please, your majesty—

SULTAN: Where are my guards?

ADORA: There aren't any.

ALADDIN *(at the same time)*: Great Sultan—

46

SULTAN: He shall die. He shall die.

ADORA *(stamping her foot)*: FATHER—listen—

SULTAN: Where are my guards? WHERE ARE MY GUARDS?????

ADORA *(looking at him till he melts before she speaks)*: There aren't any guards in my little palace, father. You can't put Prince Aladdin to death. You can't. He has saved us from the Magician who brought me here.

SULTAN: Now, Adora, don't begin talking to me about a Magician—

ALADDIN: But it was a Magician.

MOTHER: Boy, boy, don't be so foolish before the Sultan. You know there's no such thing—

SULTAN *(at the same time)*: I have never believed in Magicians, and I don't believe in them now—

(They whirl away. The Sultan says as he slows down):
What is the meaning of this Who dares to spin me like a top?

ALADDIN: It is your own thoughts that do it, sir.

MOTHER: Our thoughts?

ADORA: You need to change your mind, father. That's all. If you would both try to believe that my palace was brought here by magic—

MOTHER: How can I believe what I don't believe?

SULTAN: I never change my mind.

(They both begin to whirl, but repeat their words at once, answering each other when they become face to face with each other in their revolutions.)

MOTHER: Perhaps—

SULTAN: Do you suppose—

MOTHER: I begin to think—

SULTAN: Could I possibly be wrong? Could it possibly be true?

MOTHER *(stopping suddenly)*: Of course it's true. It's plain enough to me. How else could these things happen?

SULTAN *(half whirling in his indecision)*: It must be so—but that's believing something new—No. I can't do that. *(Whirl.)* Yes, I seem to believe it a little. I believe it in spite of myself. *(He stops and looks around in wonder.)* Have I changed my mind?

(The Magician stretches and yawns. An arm comes outside the curtain. Then he is again still. This is unnoticed by the people on the stage.)

SULTAN: How wonderful!

ADORA: I'm so glad you have. Now you'll know how brave Aladdin was. He overcame the wicked Magician all alone, and saved me from him.

(The Magician's head rises under the bottom of the curtain. He tries in vain to keep his eyes open. He sleeps on.)

SULTAN: You conquered a Magician all alone?

ALADDIN *(showing the Lamp)*: I took the magic lamp away from him and used it a little myself.

MOTHER: Why, that's the dirty lamp I wanted to sell.

ALADDIN: It brought us the food, mother.

MOTHER: I have worn and eaten magic all this time, and never knew it.
(*The palace starts with a jog. Mother screams. They all stagger at the same moment.*)

SULTAN: What's going on here? STOP THIS THING!

ADORA: We're going home, father.
(*Out the windows at the back, the stars start moving across the sky.*)

ALADDIN: See how we're rising above the clouds?

MOTHER: What if the bottom should drop out of this thing?

ALADDIN: It won't. It's a very strong palace.
(*As they stand looking out the window, the Magician stretches and yawns, rolls over drowsily, completely outside the curtains. All the others have their backs to him.*)

ADORA: Ooooooooo—how beautiful—
(*The Magician comes clear awake. He staggers to his feet. He catches sight of the lamp which Aladdin still holds, and starts for it menacingly.*)

MOTHER: Yes, it's all very lovely, but I'll be glad when we're all safe home.
(*The Magician moves steathily toward them, his eyes on Aladdin. He intends to push him out of the window. Almost ready to spring, he stops, going through the motions of getting the distance clear in his muscles. Just as he springs, Adora turns to smile up at Aladdin and sees him.*)

ADORA: Aladdin—*LOOK OUT—!!!*
(*Aladdin moves quickly. The Magician lunges at the spot where he was, cannot stop and goes out the window. Everyone cries out and springs back.*)

SULTAN: What was that?

ADORA: It was the old Magician, father. He's the one who brought me here.

ALADDIN (*jumping onto couch to look down*): He was going to push me out. Are you all right now, mother?

MOTHER: Yes, son. Just leave me alone and let me rest.

ADORA: Are you all right now, father?

SULTAN: Yes, child, I'm fine. I'll ust stay right here in this chair till we get home.

ALADDIN: We're safe, Adora. We'll never be troubled by the old Magician again.

ADORA: No, Aladdin. Never.
(*They sit quietly on a little bench down center, their backs to the audience. They look at each other and smile, and then look back toward the window and watch the stars go by as the curtain falls.*)

CURTAIN